Words on Word

Kayal Jeyaseelan

BookLeaf Publishing

India | USA | UK

Presentation by *BookLeaf Publishing*

Web: www.bookleafpub.com

E-mail: info@bookleafpub.com

ISBN: 9789363316157

First edition 2024

for everyone who makes these experiences possible.

ACKNOWLEDGEMENT

Writing poems has always been close to my heart. I owe it all to my parents, who introduced me to kids' magazines filled with small poems, transporting me to a world of my own. I can never thank them enough for opening that door. When I wrote my first poem, I shared it with my English teacher, and honestly, if she hadn't made me feel so proud, I wouldn't be where I am today. I'm grateful to all my teachers who constantly believed in me—they've been my true day ones. When I later shared my work with my friends, they were amazed, and still are. I hope to keep surprising them. I'm deeply thankful to my sister, who proofreads every poem and keeps me moving forward, and to my best friend, who reads the lore before and after every word I write. I owe thanks to everyone, including all the screens that have read my words.

I'm not sure if I can thank nature, but it's undoubtedly my greatest inspiration. Sunsets, rain, winds, and flowers—they've given me more than I could ever express.

To everyone who has played a role in my journey, thank you. I'm beyond excited to share this part of my life with you.

PREFACE

A blank document titled "ghtjd," just a random name from my keyboard, began a twenty-one-day experiment to explore the connection between my thoughts and words. What started as a simple experiment evolved into more than just writing rhyming words. I could have spent these days staring out the window or watching my favorite shows, but instead, I felt compelled to develop this new narrative style—using a Word document, no less.

I've always enjoyed writing poems, but my changing emotions every 10 minutes made it hard to put pen to paper, resulting in more uneven lines than poetry. So, I took to Microsoft for help using my not-so-favorite app, Word. While I've always found Word challenging for aligning texts and pictures, it surprisingly helped me align my thoughts seamlessly.

As you read these poems, you might notice they don't have a direct connection. That's because I draw inspiration from everyday moments—like watching my grandma make tea, my favorite loom band breaking, or rediscovering my sticker collection. Poetry has always been a way for me to transform the everyday into something meaningful, and my poems (try to) capture a snapshot of these simple yet meaningful experiences.

The thing about words is that, the other day,
I called my friend a cinnamon roll.
Golden and warm, like hugs out of the oven,
Cinnamon coughs dusted around,
Kindness swirled in layered complexities,
The gooey center, like eyes wrapped in joy,
Scent of home, gentle as they spread.
I mean, what am I saying?
Sometimes,
wonder is wrapped in simple bread.

#2

Scared I asked myself, to write or to read
my thoughts on paper, engulfed like weed.
Scared I joked, what if it's lame,
a book full of words, scars, disdain.
Scared I was to weave my stitches into words,
the needle to prick my heart, till it hurts.
Scared I was of opening the box,
memories like thread, caught by the knots.

#3

I like listening to my playlists on shuffle—
safe, knowing I didn't choose the next song.
The cautious feeling of,
"This was what was meant to be,"
where familiar and forgotten
play next to each other,
each one a comfort
in its own serendipity.

#4

I let the roses wind around me
And now I refuse to walk away
A circle of thorns surrounds me
They are small enough
I could have jumped away.

But I remained captivated, still
I chose to stay
to admire their beauty,
Come what may.
(what if Belle hadn't chosen to stay)

I let my loom band carry me home.
Loops banded tightly, keeping me safe.
Blue and white, it made me smile.
Is happiness even real if one doesn't
materialize?

#6

Today, I got a new pair of
wireless earbuds,
but my hands—
they knew the comfort of thin, insulated
copper.
They had a rhythm of their own,
a tangible familiarity.
I miss the weight of those wires,
the way they'd wrap around my fingers,
how I'd find them tangled between
my pillowcases
and soft embraces.
In the quiet spaces between
the music and calls,
I miss getting stuck
and hanging in there
on bike rides
where I don't
feel them screaming into the air.
Now I walk back home
with my hands in my pockets.
I miss those strings
and how they'd pull me back.

#7

There is something calm
about losing to people you love.
A soft surrender,
A loser but not one of sore
for in losing,
there is just something more.

You wouldn't understand.

#8

Shattered candy on the flight home,
Rust on winning medals,
Shoes worn out in travel,
glitter pens that run dry.
Nostalgia, a lie that can't be relived,
The ending of a good movie,
Films that can't be developed,
The outgrown sweater you once liked,
Holding on to a hand that will let go,
Loving something for the last time,
The sweet in bittersweet,
When yesterday sees tomorrow.

#9

The world is so big,
and time is so small,
Yet a moment stands for longer
when it's you on the call.

#10

Table for two
Coffee for one
my silent sip, a reminder
of love undone.

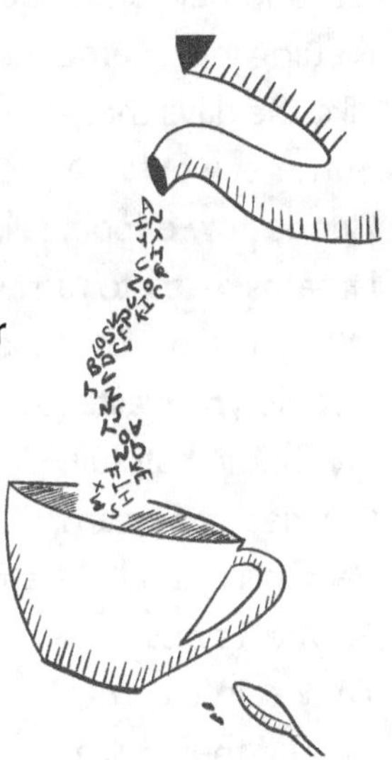

#11

I bought ice cream the other day,
Just another summer afternoon.
Melting into memories,
Like the days that would come.
Summer would be over,
Hands now dripping like
Dreams ready to run away.
I try to catch it by the cone
(Would you waste ice cream on tissues?)
My mouth half full—
Cookies and cream,
My choice is still the same.
Maybe it's best
They painfully melt.
What if they didn't,
And things got cold?
And these memories,
Frozen. (so let it go?)
Untold.

#12

If happiness was a crime,
I'd steal your smile like a shadowed gray.
A moment too would never pass,
If the hand I held could walk my way.

#13

A thousand uncounted moments,
behind these pink-lushed drapes.
Light to sweep between
Me and the world to which
my mind escapes.
Capturing my chaos
In a violet-brushed net.
Third hook a little loose,
Waves to air-conditioned breath.
Every wrinkle in the purple hem,
Strings are drawn, a second is missed,
Tomorrow is safely locked
In two curtains that perfectly kissed.

#14

The corners of my lips widen,
Like grasses grow their blades;
My thoughts unfold from narrow—
Did my cinnamon roll need more glaze?

#15

Like the cassettes at home, now gathering
dust,
I find no place to stay or to rust.
Labels too heal, then fade in silence —
But what about the laughs spent together?
Where do they go?
Tapes are tangled,
(Would you let your hair down again?)
Feelings are mixed,
I can feel the music,
A past that still sings,
In the quiet, I hear them slipping away.
But these memories that I have —
Don't let me sway.
So let's stop right here
And just press play.

#16

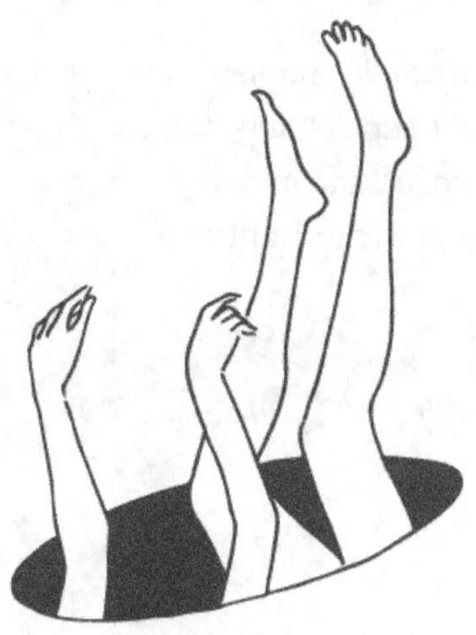

I wish I could leap
(where can I possibly find another rabbit hole?)
hope seems too far to hop to.

#17

The scent of rain-infused air
echoes of deep conversations in the mundane,
cardamom infused in tea,
there's something about those who remain.

#18

I saved those pretty stickers for later.
Who was to tell me later wouldn't come?
They sat there,
Closed in a pink glitter box.
I did peek inside,
didn't shine like the outside.
Echoed silence.
The thing is,
They won't stick anymore.
The glue faded.
There's no use trying to get them to stick.
So, I closed it up,
And sat them on the back shelf.
They'll be there.

#19

Seeking the flame in afternoon silence,
Amid casual glances from spirited flies,
Standing by grandma in her cotton silk,
Why does one wander when its milk is boiling?

With silver spoons and water clear,
I prepare another pan ready to brown,
Darkness lazing up to the metal brim,
As the gray stove slowly slows down.

For someone who is scared of heights,
I cherish this strange love for falling;
Like those colored kites
Through cut strings
Where fears lie so soft.

How is that we paint love
In the same color we bleed?
Maybe love knows pain after all—
a silent stab of crimson need.

#22

As I walk towards your casket,
And now place our cassette.
I miss playing play,
Over and over.
The candles you wished on—
Who is to answer them now?

#23

I need to stop talking to them —
the voices in my head
whispers that fill a void within
But what if they, too,
choose to tread,
Disappear beneath, the walls so thin.
I need to stop talking to them.

hope just a three-month subscription
I forgot to cancel.

#25

It's okay you couldn't care
the way that I had hoped.
Even though all I did
Was stare at your name;
despair roped.

#26

I got lost again today
Funny how I search
With yellow hope
In a clenched fist
Trying to find myself
In places I ever ceased to exist.
Anyways,
The batteries died.

There is this a thin line that weaves,
Right where the sun meets the sea
I look right where they converse
Right among the sky, sand, and me
Voices of hope
Uncertainty to glance
Tomorrow is yet to smile
And so is the chance.

#28

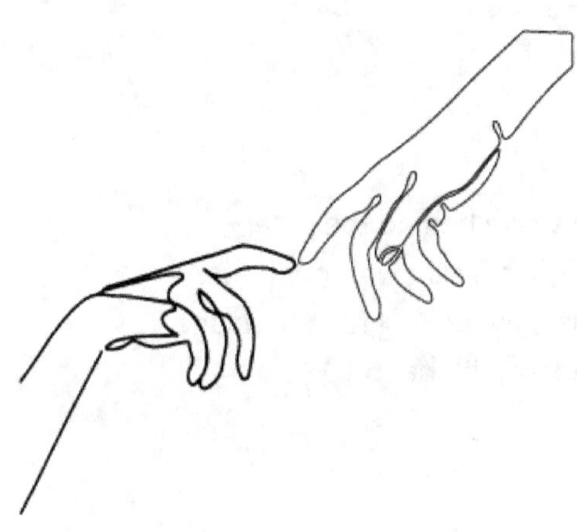

And I stood there waving at our memories
As if my fingers would bring them back.
Now, only if we could ever return,
To those days we've left behind.
I'd give you that chocolate I owed
And with it, a piece of our past,
Wrapped in the sweetness of what was,
Taste of moments we can't reclaim.

She stood behind the gate —
Peeling her skin with her tears.
I was only looking for a bandage.
Suddenly, it's been 10 years.

#30

Cotton candy
Like dreams, swirl
In summer air,
Blue or pink,
Choosing
Doesn't seem fair.

When books close,
we meet in the folds.

Narratives conclude,
yet these pages hold.
In binding's crease,
these impressions linger,
ink traces stories
on my fingers.

#32

I can hear talking,
But I can also —
Hear
goosebumps whispering,
Bicycle bells,
Pen on paper,
Fresh tears falling,
Pages turning,
Wind rustling,
Heartbeats,
Moments,
Unseen,
Unheard,
Yet deeply felt.

#33

My feet are on the ground
I know I'm meant to stay
The pulse on my feet.
Periwinkle roots entwine,
gentle threads through soil and time.
In this embrace of earth and vine,
I meant to say—these moments
are wholly mine.

#34

Me, my slippers, and my peach iced tea
5 am in the morning
sea blue, copper blue,
my face changes
pink to orange to yellow
my thoughts float in
you, me, and some peach iced tea.

#35

A simple scar,
Browned so fast.
Longing
To be painted upon,
By the canvas of memories
That drives them.

#36

sunset behind my ears,
starlight in my eyes,
whispers of the air,
my jhumka dangles twice.

#37

How easy
Stuffed cotton feels—
How safe.
Soft fur whispers
Fuzzy secrets shared,
in button eyes
that always cared.
In the warmth of cuddles,
we learn, love
that's stitched together,
one teddy bear at a time.

#38

So here I stood
With a paintbrush in my hand,
Watercolors on the beach,
My feet are buried in the sand.
I dipped my brush into the sea,
Drawing colors from the waves,
With hues of me on the one before,
Painting thoughts that someone saved—
Worn footprints washed ashore.

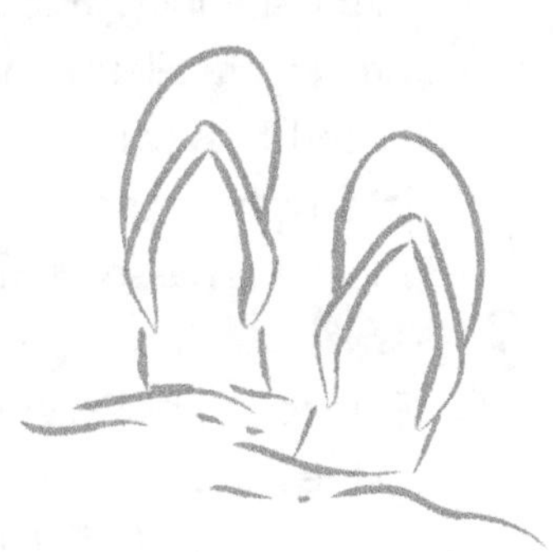

There is an ache on the edge of seventeen
In the scribbles long outgrown
Broken bracelets and pink diaries
Friendships written in classroom seats,
late-night talks and whispered hopes,
the notes passed in hidden code.

Perhaps it's not in what's left behind,
In the boxes where I packed my life,
I'll still have a KitKat in my bag
Where it'll always be for me to find.

#40

I guess that's why
they are called wishes—
blown away on candles,
and lashes.

dandelion seeds soar,
never to land.

#41

It's 5:37, doors close at six,
The lamppost flickers, shadows stick.
Hues of calm, jumps, and laughter.
trampoline parks, tooth fairies drifting after
Tranquil paints in rhythmic slow,
all for these dusted memories to let go.

#42

the warmth of the morning sun,
sand between my toes,
the scent of rain on a summer day,
fireflies on a warm night,
the taste of fresh-picked berries,
freshly opened book,
the echo of familiar songs,
joy of a shared secret,
the smile that follows tears,
promise standing years
the hugs in an airport,
soft smiles in a graveyard.

A simple list
Of silence kissed.

#43

Think about life like a video game.
Sometimes the control slips through
And sometimes, the wrong button
Yet maybe, just maybe
takes you to the right place.

#44

Smells of Nostalgia

Empty play-doh of molded dreams,
Chocolate swirls on vanilla ice creams.
Capri Sun, strawberry sweet,
Watermelons in summer heat.
Tiffin boxes, warmed by the sun,
Kool-Aid wipes after sweaty runs.
Fruity pencil erasers, fresh grass,
The not-so-quiet snacks in class.
Lilies laid on bed sheets yawning,
The smell of Sunday on a Monday morning.

#45

The thing about ending video calls
Is that I feel the sudden space
Between the red button
And my hand.
Is that the space feels wider,
Fingers hover, hesitant,
Over buttons.
The room returns to silence,
The ghost of connection remains.

#46

But if you think about it,
All you need is some
smiles around you,
morning coffee,
and a good view.
Deep conversations,
presence,
absence,
light,
fresh air,
sun there,
and some tea to brew.

I stick these pieces into the mosaic
my mind is,
wondering if it's a strength or weakness
to hold on to these relics of us.

Perhaps the answer lies in not forgetting.

#48

Missing people,
at three in the afternoon.
Missing a roof,
a hand,
a shoulder.
Letting go is something—
suddenly,
I'm older.

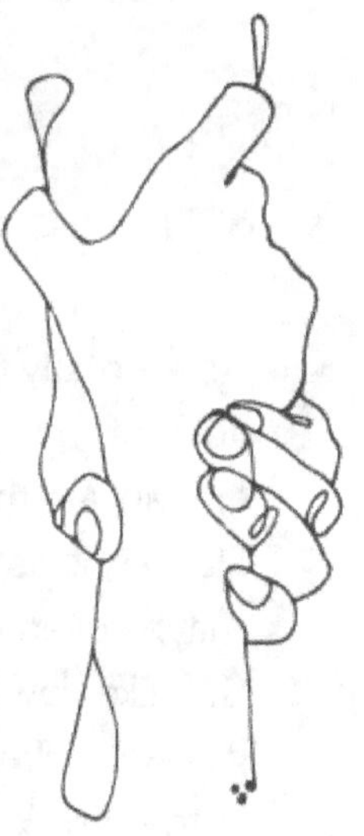

#49

Accidentally thought about the
color of my eyes.
I mean, are they just brown? Chocolate brown?
Dark chocolate, but
maybe even the right coffee brown.
Soft like how autumn leaves fall,
glass-like river tops,
in the sun like honey, dripping.
And when the light hits,
a hint of amber, warm—
a shade of brown, forever new.
Silent, unknown, but not untrue.

#50

Funny how I'd
Write some people in the same font,
Bold, *italicized,*
<u>Underlined with lies.</u>

Tears crash like waves
waves feel like hugs
salt and water
silent tugs.

Soft pulls at the heart's shore,
sixty percent water and rest downpour.

#52

My body with the earth,
messages with the stars.
(The sky is clear.)
My head feels cold,
Unforgiving,
Restless for thoughts to keep.
I can hear the honks,
The echoes,
With nothing to seep
(Unless tears count.)
The cracks.
My fingers,
Stuck between the fragments of my
imagination
And the dawning sense of reality.

We need more of
short story long,
carving shapes in the sky,
flowers pressed in books,
cards that have hugs,
the delicate web of dreams,
and the undeniable weight of truth.
Bridging the gap between what is
and what could be,
we find ourselves
where dreams touch hope,
written in constellations.

#54

The real question is when to stop
Reading these letters I have,
Ink faded, but emotions still wave.
Liking the same color you did,
shades that paint memories vivid.
Adding songs to these playlists old,
Each note is a reminder musically told.

So,
Is that it?
Conceit—
we must meet apart.
Yet, even in separation,
Your presence
a shadow in my thoughts.

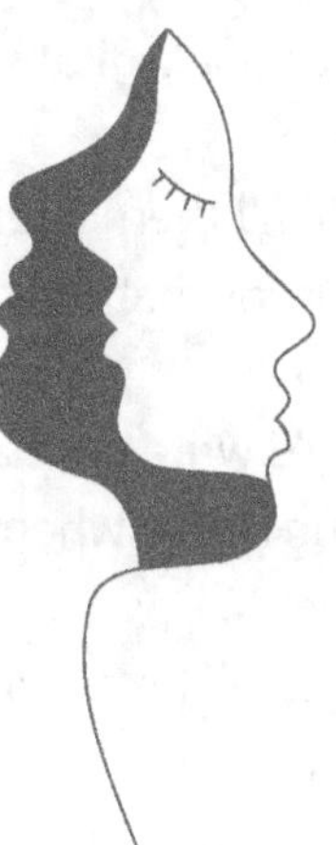

In scrapbooks that still have paper,
I wonder,
what'll fill them later.
With pens that miss their caps,
I wonder,
if they'd write on maps,
leading me to when I didn't know how to,
maybe,
Life was all better without a future in my sight.
I wonder,
if I'd find them again when
my hands are stained in ink.

#56

I wish flowers knew how much
We adored them, how they—
How they'd just press between books,
Especially those bougainvilleas,
Pink and full of promises.
Jasmine entwined within my braids
As they weave through the strands of my hair.
I'd sleep through sunrise
And they'd still be locked right there.
And these roses—
I know they have thorns,
But everyone likes roses.
Beauty often adorns
Even where pain imposes.

I hold these flowers in my hand.
To hand them out to you;
I know it doesn't make up for everything,
But here is a part of me—that's annoyingly true.

And Lilies—
Yeah, I like them.
Don't know why.

#57

I find my childhood
in these textures.
Wrapped in biscuits and hard toffee,
Tiramisu, chocolate, and cold coffee.
Scraped knees and band-aids,
Muddy feet and messy braids.
Sketch pens and hidden ink,
Barbie dolls and memories pink.
Little stars and rainbow fishes,
Birthday cakes and frosting wishes.
Secret forts and pillow fights,
Summer breezes and ice cream nights.
Laughter shared and merry-go-rounds
Tear down my cheeks to hug it all out.

#58

I love wrapping gifts in
Small cardboard boxes cloaked in brown
paper,
In a texture that balances between
Soft tissue and graham crackers.
Secrets between folds
Crinkled newspaper to rustle with emotions,
Not just of things, but of thoughts,
White chocolate tucked within,
With words that embrace like a long hug.
Colored pens and a free hand drawing
A red-striped ribbon,
A careful knot to keep it all safe—
I mean, it's red.
A piece of my heart.
So here you go
Together apart.

*Just letting my heart overflow
(like ink from pen
like chocolate drizzle on vanilla cake
like splattered orange on canvas white)*

you are worth the mess.

#60

Then all I had left was my Pinterest board—
a collection of me,
disorganized,
a mosaic of moments and dreams,
waiting to be edited.
When life turns difficult,
I have a place to
Archive myself,
finding solace in the familiar,
saved,
hanging on to the threads.
An average Pinterest user,
seeking comfort in curated chaos,
clarity among the clutter,
piecing myself together,
one pin at a time.

#61

It was four in the afternoon,
And we were playing Snakes and Ladders.
I rolled the dice
And climbed up a snake
Heard irony laugh
So I slid down,
Pretty smooth.

Rainbows, a purple promise,
clinging on to me.
Three little stars,
like the ones in school,
ready to be stamped,
admired by eager eyes.
Washed away,
but not forgotten.

#63

I sit with songs playing on my laptop,
Confidently singing wrong words
They are there, clear and sharp,
But you see,
I prefer to read between the lines, unheard.
Much like feelings, never as they seem,
Acknowledging the truth yet drifting by,
In a world of delusions, I craft my sky.

Where misheard melodies form,
the soundtrack of my life.

I'm a puzzle piece lost to the back of my sofa.
I'm certain it's there.
It's just something I can't find.
I'm still not used to picking up fallen pieces.

$$\#65$$

Somehow,
The best goodbye hugs
Are the ones not shared,
Replayed endlessly in your mind
Until they finally walk away.
Words caught in your throat,
Heavy—
But not more than this heart,
Embrace now just a word
Lingering in the space
That once held us close.

But in these quiet goodbyes,
When curtains fall,
I'll find my way backstage,
To you.

#66

You know it's suddenly six,
Six, even, unlike my mind,
The sky blushes pink,
Unbothered, hot, sweet, and cruel,
Not entirely at peace, yet not quite blue.
Streetlights dance to life,
As the world around me softly fades.

In the embrace of trees and shadows,
The air is still warm, summer is still sought,
Moods drift like leaves, thoughts trailing like
ants.

Cats slip, barely more than these hands,
Lingering around, yet my feet still stand.
In my gaze, paused, suspended in the crescent
unmoved,
Yet these ripples on the water stay restless,
Dappling with the stars above.
(Pocahontas whispers the colors of the wind)

The truth is, today,
Eight billion people experienced life different
This month is to end
Last year, just a few moments ago
Next month is right around the corner
Sand in the hourglass shattered.

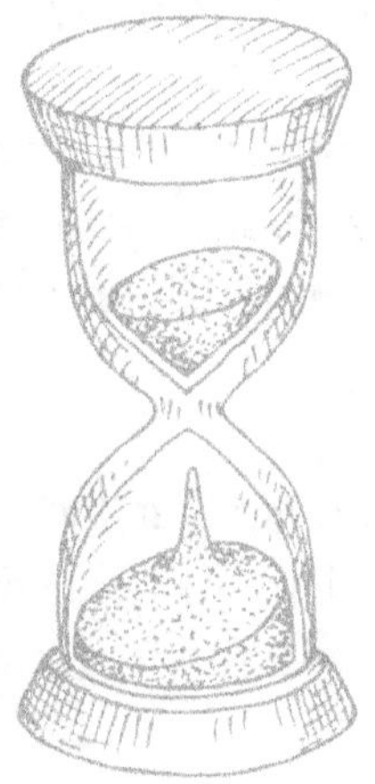

Nostalgia only lies.

#68

Things for college.

Wide-leg jeans,
Journals for thoughts,
(we need more than one)
Fragments of faraway friendships,
(letters in a clear file)
Late-night snacks,
(best shared)
Whispers to the sky,
(Hopes and dreams)
A map of my songs,
(Playlists from 2016)
A cozy blanket,
(Amma's dupatta)
Two pens
One black, one blue.

and myself.

#69

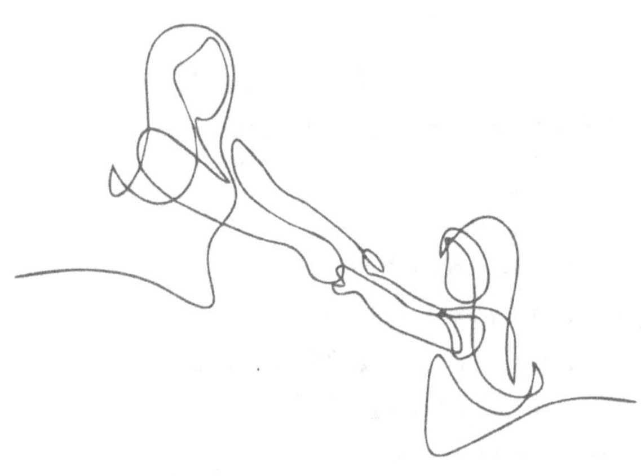

In airports with big clocks,
Running belts at the conveyor,
Airport hugs, the best of the worst,
But I'm wondering what's next.
Announcements breaking through the air,
A mix of excitement, a touch of fear,
With a placard in my hand,
And my mind at those gates,
faces passing by,
Arrivals on big green plates,
Soon we'll stand on this side.

(my sister came back home today.)

#70

Then on a random Thursday,
We stepped out as a class,
Together, for the last time.
It's the summer before college.
Everything is going to change.

Even if days don't seem that far,
The sun shined longer
When they circled around.
These memories are still warm,
Like the school jackets we shared.
Not more than the hugs,
But letting this go,
Was there some textbook to prepare?

So here we are,
With our handprints in blue,
Pasting them on ruled paper,
Without any hopes anew.
Caps, gowns, pencils, pens—
Fifth grade was long ago,
So why does it feel like we are ten?

Now we wait,
In moments captured in reverse,
Looking through the frames,
With these faces hidden in my purse.
Feelings lingering in the background,
It's only time.
We leave.
Now when we next meet,
We can only hope we are
Forever seventeen.

For now,
It's hard to say goodbye.

#71

Words without causes,
Dependent clauses,
Incomplete fragments,
Thoughts find their pauses.
In the quiet of a document,
These everyday moments aligned,
In skies and seas blue,
Almost finding a meaning.
In Unworded words.
Locked memories glued.